Who Is the Holy Spirit?

A Guide to
the Holy Spirit

Who Is the
Holy Spirit?

Basic Bible Studies
for Everyone

HARVEST HOUSE PUBLISHERS
EUGENE, OREGON

WHO IS THE HOLY SPIRIT?
Stonecroft Bible Studies
Copyright © 2012 by Stonecroft Ministries, Inc.
www.stonecroft.org
Published by Harvest House Publishers
Eugene, Oregon 97402
www.harvesthousepublishers.com

ISBN 978-0-7369-5193-7 (pbk.)
ISBN 978-0-7369-5194-4 (eBook)

Printed in the United States of America

12 13 14 15 16 17 18 19 20 / VP-CD / 10 9 8 7 6 5 4 3 2 1

Contents

||||||||||||||||||||||||||||

Acknowledgments

Stonecroft wishes to acknowledge Janice Mayo Mathers for her dedication in serving the Lord through Stonecroft. Speaker, author, and National Board Member, Jan is the primary author of revised Stonecroft Bible Studies. We appreciate her love for God's Word and her love for people who need Him. Stonecroft also thanks the team who surrounded Jan in prayer, editing, design, and creative input to make these studies accessible to all.

Welcome to
Stonecroft Bible Studies!

At Stonecroft, we connect you with God, each other, and your communities.

It doesn't matter where you've been or what you've done... God wants to be in relationship with you. And one place He tells you about Himself is in His Word—the Bible. Whether the Bible is familiar or new to you, its contents will transform your life and bring answers to your biggest questions.

Gather with people in your community—women, men, couples, young and old alike—and explore together what the Bible says about the Holy Spirit. This study will reveal who He is, what He does, and how your life will be completely different with Him.

Each chapter includes discussion questions to stir up meaningful conversation, specific Scripture verses to investigate, and time for prayer to connect with God and each other.

Discover more of God and His ways through this small-group exploration of the Bible.

Tips for Using This Study

This book has several features that make it easy to use and helpful for your life:

- The page number or numbers given after every Bible reference are keyed to the page numbers in the *Abundant Life Bible*. This handy paperback Bible uses the New Living Translation, a recent version in straightforward, up-to-date language. We encourage you to obtain a copy through your group leader or at stonecroft.org.

- Each chapter ends with a section called "Thoughts, Notes, and Prayer Requests." Use this space for notes or for thoughts that come to you during your group time or study, as well as prayer requests.

- In the back of the book you will find "Journal Pages"—a space available for writing down how the study is changing your life or any other personal thoughts, reactions, and reflections.

- Please make this book and study your own. We encourage you to use it and mark it in any way that helps you grow in your relationship with God!

If you find this study helpful, you may want to investigate other resources from Stonecroft. Please take a look at "Stonecroft Resources" in the back of the book or online at stonecroft.org/store.

stonecroft.org

1

Knowing the Holy Spirit's Presence

They were just ordinary men, fishermen by trade. However, after observing Jesus perform miracles like healings, exorcisms, and then bringing an abundance of fish to their nets after hours of receiving none, the men left everything and followed Jesus. They become Jesus' first disciples—the first "Christ-followers."

They and the other disciples who joined them asked Jesus all of the questions that arose in their minds; however, Jesus' answers weren't always as they expected. Yet they couldn't stop following Him, because He was like no one else they had ever known. He was a man, yet He claimed He was God's Son. He performed miracles and talked with great wisdom and authority. The disciples did not always understand what Jesus said or why He had said it, but they still wanted to be with Him wherever He went, whatever the cost.

The disciples followed Jesus for several years and tried to soak in all of His wisdom and teaching. As a result, they became close. Jesus told His disciples several times about His coming death. He angered the wrong people, so the religious leaders devised a plot to kill Him—and succeeded. Yet their plot was part of God's overall sovereign plan for Jesus to bring salvation through His death and resurrection, so that His people can be with Him forever. In the meantime, however, He has left earth so that He can prepare a place for His followers.

As Jesus' time on earth drew to a close, the disciples felt the tension building all around them. If you read all of John 14, you will see how Jesus did all He could to make the coming days as bearable as possible for His beloved disciples. He wanted to prepare them for the days ahead when He would no longer be physically present with them. In John 14:1-17 (page 823) He explained His plan to leave.

"Don't let your hearts be troubled. Trust in God, and trust also in me. There is more than enough room in my Father's home. If this were not so, would I have told you that I am going to prepare a place for you? When everything is ready, I will come and get you, so that you will always be with me where I am. And you know the way to where I am going."

"No, we don't know, Lord," Thomas said. "We have no idea where you are going, so how can we know the way?"

Jesus told him, "I am the way, the truth, and the life. No one can come to the Father except through me. If you had really known me, you would know who my Father is. From now on, you do know him and have seen him!"

Philip said, "Lord, show us the Father, and we will be satisfied."

Jesus replied, "Have I been with you all this time, Philip, and yet you still don't know who I am? Anyone who has seen me has seen the Father! So why are you asking me to show him to you? Don't you believe that I am in the Father and the Father is in me? The words I speak are not my own, but my Father who lives in me does his work through me. Just believe that I am in the Father and the Father is in me. Or at least believe because of the work you have seen me do.

"I tell you the truth, anyone who believes in me will do the same works I have done, and even greater works, because I am going to be with the Father. You can ask for anything in my name, and I will do it, so that the Son can bring glory to the Father. Yes, ask me for anything in my name, and I will do it!

"If you love me, obey my commandments. And I will ask

the Father, and he will give you another Advocate, who will never leave you. He is the Holy Spirit, who leads into all truth. The world cannot receive him, because it isn't looking for him and doesn't recognize him. But you know him, because he lives with you now and later will be in you."

Prayer

Father, my heart has heard you say to come and talk with you, and that's what I'm doing. You gave me Jesus as the way to you, to show me who you are, and as an example to follow and learn truth from. In His absence, you now have given me your Holy Spirit, who leads me into all truth. Please teach me and guide me today as I look at the Spirit's role in my life (Psalm 27:8, page 425, and John 14:16-18, page 823).

In His conversation with the disciples in John 14, which dealt with His plan to leave, Jesus told them about the Holy Spirit. *"Remember,"* He said to them, *"my words are not my own. What I am telling you is from the Father who sent me. I am telling you these things now while I am still with you. But when the Father sends the Advocate as my representative—that is, the Holy Spirit—he will teach you everything and will remind you of everything I have told you"* (John 14:24-26, pages 823-824).

> The spiritual life is always a surrendered life where the Holy Spirit is our most valuable resource.
>
> — *Gail E. Dudley*

Notice how Jesus assured the disciples several times that they wouldn't be alone, that Someone would come after He was gone. He called this Person by two different names. Read John 14:26 (pages 823-824).

What are those names?

What comes to mind when you think of the word *advocate*?

Merriam-Webster's Collegiate Dictionary defines *advocate* as "one that pleads the cause of another." Isn't it wonderful to know that God has given us an Advocate so we are never alone in this life? We always have someone who is sticking up for us!

As we look closer, we learn that the word translated *Advocate* is also translated as *Helper* or *Comforter.* Whatever the translation, they all go back to same Greek word, the meaning being someone who comes alongside to help or support—or in a legal sense, someone doing work on behalf of someone else. The Holy Spirit is our Advocate, who brings rebirth and renewal to our spirit. The Holy Spirit is our Helper, who comes to our aid and makes God's presence real to us. The Holy Spirit is our Comforter, who gives us peace and strength when we are hurting. The Holy Spirit is always in us to offer assistance, encouragement, and help.

Have you ever had someone you considered to be your advocate? How did they help you?

God Is One

Besides *Advocate,* the other name Jesus called His representative in John 14 was the *Holy Spirit.* This name is a little more difficult to understand, isn't it? A spirit does not have a physical body like Jesus did when He lived on earth, but there is a clear connection between Him and the Holy Spirit. In fact, in John 14 Jesus repeatedly connects all three Persons—Jesus, the Son; God the Father; and the Holy Spirit. Read John 14:16-20 (page 823).

Who did Jesus ask to send the Holy Spirit?

Why did Jesus say the disciples already knew the Holy Spirit?

Where did Jesus say He would live later?

At the time when Jesus was speaking to them, He said the Holy Spirit was *with* them. But after Jesus was gone, He said the Holy Spirit would live *in* them. What is the connection?

The names and titles of the Holy Spirit reveal His relationship to God the Father and to Jesus Christ. Read Romans 8:9 (page 862).

What two names are given here?

Now see what Jesus said in John 10:30 (page 819):

The Bible indicates throughout that God the Father, Jesus the Son, and the Holy Spirit are one Being. We often refer to all three as the Trinity. We have one God who is three different Persons. They are co-equal, co-existent, and co-eternal. Therefore, the Holy Spirit is God, and He possesses all the attributes of Deity.

Does this seem hard to understand? How can One be Three, and Three be One? God is so wonderful that His greatness cannot be described or grasped by our finite minds. One of the reasons God sent Jesus to earth was to reveal God's nature and greatness in a way we could understand. When we trust Jesus as our Savior, God gives us His Spirit to live in us, guide us, and teach us more about God.

The more we read and study God's Word and the more time we spend with Him, the more we'll begin to understand the oneness of the Father, the Son, and the Holy Spirit.

The Purposes of the Holy Spirit

The Trinity is the three Persons of the Deity—Father, Son, and Holy Spirit—yet they are still one God. Each has specific functions in our lives. Out of the three, it may be the most difficult for us to visualize the Holy Spirit. The Spirit is the One who is our intimate companion, making Christ's presence real to us. He brings us to the truth about Jesus and leads us to salvation. He empowers us to live our daily lives. He speaks to us. He leads us. He prays for us. He teaches us. He is, in fact, our Advocate in every aspect of our life.

Read the following verses and record how the Spirit actively engages us in our lives.

Acts 13:2 (page 841)

Romans 8:26 (page 862)

Romans 8:14 (page 862)

John 15:26 (page 824)

John 14:26 (pages 823-824)

Do you see how the Holy Spirit is more than a vague spiritual force? He has distinct things He does for us.

The Holy Spirit has another purpose, this one directed to all those in the world who don't know God. Read John 16:7-11 (page 824). What will the Spirit convict the world of?

God's desire is to be in close relationship with every person, but sin interferes with that. It's the Holy Spirit who makes people aware of sin and separation from God so they can turn to Him, the One who removes the barrier. The Bible tells us that the result of sin is spiritual death and eventual judgment. As Advocate, the Spirit wants the same thing that the Father wants, which is that everyone would repent and turn to Him. The Holy Spirit kindly reveals sin to humanity. He makes all people aware—no matter how much they want to remain in denial—that without Him they will one day face judgment.

Let's read what the Bible says about judgment in Jude 1:14-16 (page 947). What is the Lord returning to do?

What is the punishment of sin, according to Romans 6:23 (page 861)?

The Bible says we cannot enter God's Kingdom unless we have received new birth through the Holy Spirit, the gift of eternal life. An important role of the Spirit is making us aware of our sin so we can receive that free gift.

Once we have received the gift of the new birth, the Holy Spirit continues to help us face our sin. Read Romans 8:12-14 (page 862).

What is the Spirit's role in helping you deal with sin?

If we are led by the Spirit—and that includes putting to death sinful deeds—we know we are children of God. Isn't that amazing? We aren't alone in facing sin in our lives!

Read Psalm 139:1-7 and 23-24 (pages 476-477).

Why is it a good thing that God knows everything about you?

The Indwelling of God's Spirit

When we believe that Jesus' death on the cross was the full payment for our sins, God forgives our sins and takes control of our lives. At that moment, we receive His Holy Spirit into our lives and are born into God's family. From that point on, the Spirit is always in us and gives us guidance every day. Read the following verses to see how we are born into God's family.

John 3:5-7 (page 811)

Titus 3:4-7 (page 918)

Do you see the vital role the Holy Spirit plays in making a relationship with God possible? The moment we realize our hopeless condition of being separated from God and ask Him to save us, we receive His free gift of salvation and we are reborn through the Holy Spirit, who enters our life.

Now read John 3:16 (page 811) and Revelation 22:17 (page 962) to see who can receive this gift. (Note: *Bride* means the church—all those who have received Jesus as their Savior and Lord.)

Read Romans 8:2,10 (page 862).

What has freed us from the power of sin?

Read Hebrews 9:14 (page 925).

In whose power did Christ offer Himself as a sacrifice for our sins?

While we know that God desires everyone to be in relationship with Him, not everyone responds. He gave us free will, and no matter how strongly He desires to have a relationship with us, He will not force it. Accepting Jesus as our Savior is a conscious act of our will—nothing else. The result is that God takes our sin-filled life and exchanges it for a new life in Christ. At that moment, the Holy Spirit indwells you—makes His home inside you—empowering this new life. Through Him, God the Father creates a new heart within you. Old things and old ways are past, and a new life begins!

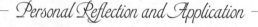

Personal Reflection and Application

From this chapter,

I see...

I believe...

I will...

Prayer

Father, help me to give myself to you because of all you have given to me—especially the Holy Spirit, my Advocate. Because He is in me, let me be a living and holy sacrifice—the kind you will find acceptable. Don't let me copy the behavior and customs of this world. Instead, transform me into a new person by changing the way I think, so that I will learn to know your good and perfect will for me (Romans 12:1-2, page 866).

———— *Thoughts, Notes, and Prayer Requests* ————

2

What Is the Holy Spirit's Work?

I was at a stoplight, looking down at my shopping list, when my foot slipped off the brake and I rolled into the car in front of me. As soon as the light turned green, the other driver and I pulled into a nearby parking lot to assess the damage. The man examined his car and then mine. "I don't see any damage," he said, "so I think we're okay."

"Let me give you my insurance card, just in case," I said.

He examined his vehicle again, this time more closely. "Not necessary. Everything looks okay." At my insistence he took my card, and we went our separate ways.

The next thing I know, I'm served notice that I'm being sued for $150,000 in damages and injuries.

I was astounded! He wouldn't even have had my name if I hadn't insisted. Now here were photos of major damage to his vehicle and doctor bills showing extensive neck injuries. The blatant lies and injustice filled me with helpless anger.

My insurance agent smiled calmly. "You have nothing to worry about," she said. "We'll take care of this, and you're not going to be out any time or money. Relax and let us handle it."

How wonderful to have an advocate—someone who would fight my battle, protect me from the injustice, and pay my bill. Of course, I pay my insurance company a monthly fee to be my advocate. My true Advocate—the Holy Spirit—doesn't require a monthly payment. My true Advocate fights for me out of pure love.

Prayer

God, I am so thankful that you—Father, Son, and Spirit— are the same throughout both the Old and New Testaments, for you are unchanging. I pray that you will show me how your Spirit worked in the past and how He works in my life today (John 14:7, page 823, and John 15:26, page 824).

God's Spirit in the Old Testament

We are introduced to the Holy Spirit in the very first book of the Bible—Genesis. Read Genesis 1:2 (page 3).

What did the Holy Spirit do?

Let's look at some other references to the Holy Spirit and the role He played in people's lives. After each reference, note what He is called and what He does.

Job 33:4 (page 408)

Ezekiel 36:27 (page 655)

Micah 3:8 (page 705)

2 Samuel 23:2 (page 254)

In chapter 1, we learned about some of the roles the Spirit plays in our lives today. How does what He did in these Old Testament references relate to those roles?

It's interesting to note that it's David, the man who wrote many of the psalms, speaking in 2 Samuel 23:2 (page 254). The Holy Spirit inspired David to write the words that have comforted and challenged people for thousands of years!

Just as with David and others, the Holy Spirit is always working in and through us in various ways, just as He chooses. Whatever it may be—whether big or small—don't forget to give credit to whom credit is due. With reflection and prayer, you will know in what areas the Spirit has been working in your life.

Can you name a few of those areas right now?

We have looked at the role of the Holy Spirit in creation and His role in various people's lives. Let's look more at what the Old Testament has to say about the Holy Spirit.

Read Isaiah 11:2 (page 525). List the different ways the Spirit is referred to.

Look at your list: wisdom, understanding, counsel, might, knowledge, and fear of the Lord. This passage is referring to the Spirit's work in Jesus, but it is the same Spirit who can impart all of these things to you as you have need. They aren't things that you receive all at once when you are saved—they come as you spend more time getting to know and trust God, reading the Bible, and in conversation with Him.

The Old Testament shows us that sometimes the Holy Spirit came upon certain people to enable them to fulfill a certain task God gave them. For example, He gave the Holy Spirit to help Bezalel be a master craftsman who was empowered to work on the tabernacle. Read Exodus 31:3 (page 69).

The Holy Spirit also provided certain Old Testament people with unusual physical strength, military skills, and the abilities needed to lead a nation. For example, the Spirit came powerfully upon David when he was anointed to be king (1 Samuel 16:13, page 223).

The Holy Spirit in the New Testament

Even though there are accounts of the Holy Spirit at work in the Old Testament, far more is revealed about Him in the New Testament. We learn from Jesus about the Holy Spirit entering a person and dwelling with them forever. Read John 14:16 (page 823). We are also told that the Spirit is "poured out." He is now available to all believers all the time.

The fact that the Holy Spirit now indwells believers permanently is the major difference between the Holy Spirit's work in the Old Testament and the New Testament. Interestingly, there is no recorded activity of the Holy Spirit during the 400 years between the last book of the Old Testament and the first book of the New Testament. During this same time, there were no prophets speaking God's words. Then suddenly, the Holy Spirit began an active ministry, preparing for the coming of Jesus Christ.

The Holy Spirit in the Life of Christ

From Jesus' conception to His ascension, He was continually led by the Holy Spirit. Read the following verses and note the part the Spirit played in each circumstance.

Matthew 1:18-20 (page 733)

Luke 4:1 (page 783)

Luke 4:16-19 (pages 783-784)

Romans 8:11 (page 862)

Acts 1:1-2 (page 830)

Although Jesus, who is God the Son, had the power to do these things on His own, He placed Himself under the same human limitations we have, choosing instead to be under the control of the Holy Spirit in order to reveal to us how we can do the same. He set the example for us, showing us how God wants us to live. And as the Holy Spirit guided Jesus, He will guide and enable us as we listen to and respond to Him.

The Holy Spirit's Role in Writing the Bible

Read 2 Peter 1:20-21 (page 938).

Who told the people who wrote the Bible what to write?

From whom did the message come?

Read 1 Corinthians 2:13-14 (page 871).

What is the significance of Paul using the Spirit's words to explain spiritual truths?

Read 2 Peter 1:21 (page 938) again.

Who gave the Holy Spirit the words?

This is why the Bible is often called *God's Word*. The Holy Spirit had men write the words God gave them.

How might the statement in the sidebar change how you experience the Bible as you are reading it?

Imagine God sitting beside you as you read His Word, His communication to you. Have you ever stopped to consider that even right this moment, as we are discussing what the Bible says, God the Author is listening in? And not only that, but the Holy Spirit is calling certain phrases to our attention that He knows we need. The Holy Spirit is always working on our behalf!

> The Bible is the only book whose author is present whenever it is read.

The Holy Spirit in Our Lives

The Holy Spirit has two main areas in our lives in which He actively works. First, He reveals God to us and regenerates us. That is, He is the one through whom we are born again. Read the following verses to see the Spirit's involvement in our salvation.

> To be *regenerated* and to be *born again* are similar in what they mean.

John 6:63 (page 815) and John 3:6-7 (page 811)

This is why, when someone commits their life to Christ, they often say they have been "born again."

Second, the Holy Spirit is God with us and in us, and He continually reveals God to us as He teaches us and guides us. Summarize the following verses.

1 Corinthians 2:10-12 (page 871)

According to verse 11, who knows God's thoughts?

How does this show the oneness of the Father, the Son, and the Holy Spirit?

Through the Holy Spirit we can know God's deep secrets! What an incredible level of intimacy with Him is available to us! Think of the person you are most intimate with in this entire world. Do you know their thoughts or their deep secrets? You may *assume* what their thoughts are, based on your familiarity, but unless they tell you their thoughts or share their secrets with you, you can only guess at them. But God doesn't want you guessing. He makes Himself fully available to you through His Spirit.

Read 2 Corinthians 1:21-22 (page 882) and Romans 8:15-16 (page 862) to see another purpose the Holy Spirit has.

What proves we belong to God?

What does Paul say that the Holy Spirit is?

What happens at the same time we receive God's Spirit?

Wow—don't you love that? The Holy Spirit assures us that we are children of God.

Take a moment to think about it. So much has now been made available to us because of the Holy Spirit. Through Him we have received eternal life, the same kind of life God has. Through Him we have a close, personal relationship with God. Through Him we know we are part of God's own family. But there's more!

The Spirit is also our Teacher. Read John 14:15-17,26 (pages 823-824).

What will the Spirit lead you into?

What will He teach you?

Read John 16:13-15 (pages 824-825).

Whose words will the Spirit speak to you?

The Spirit receives the words to speak to us from Jesus Himself. Who does Jesus receive the words from to pass on to the Spirit to pass on to us?

The Guidance of the Spirit

The Holy Spirit not only teaches us and reminds us of truth, but He also guides us. He enables us to accomplish God's plan for our lives. We don't know what our future holds, but because the Holy Spirit, God Himself, is living in us, we have nothing to fear. If we give

Him full access to our lives and trust Him to lead us, we will be the person God designed us to be, regardless of circumstances or events in our lives that try to destroy that.

However, it is very easy to fall into the trap of living our life according to other people's expectations rather than God's.

What problems can it cause when we try to live up to other people's expectations?

Those are precisely the pitfalls the Holy Spirit, as your personal Advocate, wants to help you avoid. And this is where you have to be alert. As we've already said, God isn't going to interfere with your free will, so though the Holy Spirit is your Advocate, He is not your jailer. He will guide you, but He will not force you. He will not shove or drag you. It may be helpful rather to think of His guidance as nudges or gentle tugs.

Have you ever felt the Holy Spirit guiding you?

Describe a time in your life when you knew the Holy Spirit was guiding you.

The way to grow in your ability to differentiate between your self-will and God's will is to spend consistent time in conversation and close communion with Him and in reading your Bible, because one of the ways God speaks to us is through His Word, the Bible. The Bible is full of real-life stories of people who have struggled with the same things we struggle with today: hatred, conflict, jealousy, out-of-bounds sexual desire, relationship issues, greed, aloneness, a stagnant spiritual life, and so on. From front to back, the Bible reveals God's redemptive story of His people—a story of His love, justice, joy, and pain as people choose to either listen to Him or refuse to listen.

The Bible is full of God's ways for your life. If a desire is in opposition to what His Word says, don't do it. The Holy Spirit will always be nudging you and bringing to your memory everything Christ told us. The closer you stay to God, the more familiar you will become with those nudges and tugs and the more you will be able to trust them.

If you feel the need to rationalize a decision or action you want to take, stop and think. You are probably heading in the wrong direction. The Holy Spirit's direction should not require any rationalization.

Can you think of a time you rationalized a decision you later regretted?

Through the guidance of the Holy Spirit and following the teachings of the Bible, you will avoid hindrances to God's best, unique, and creative plan for your life. As God becomes the true center of your life more and more and as you learn to love Him with your whole heart, your thoughts will naturally align more with His. You will discover that your life will become more meaningful. The people around you will see the change in your purpose for living.

In closing, read Galatians 5:16 (page 893). What happens when we allow the Holy Spirit to guide our lives? Share from your life experience.

In what area of your life do you feel you most need the Spirit's guidance right now?

Take a few minutes to write out a prayer stating your need.

Now take some time to listen to what the Holy Spirit is saying to you.

———— *Personal Reflection and Application* ————

From this chapter,

I see...

I believe...

I will...

Prayer

Father, because of your glory and excellence, you have given me great and precious promises that enable me to share in your divine nature and escape the world's corruption caused by human desires. Thank you for your promise to guide me along the best pathway for my life and to advise me and watch over me (2 Peter 1:4, page 938, and Psalm 32:8, page 427).

Thoughts, Notes, and Prayer Requests

_____

_____

_____

_____

_____

_____

_____

_____

_____

_____

_____

_____

_____

_____

_____

_____

_____

_____

3

How Does the Holy Spirit
Help Me Grow?

The instructions were simple. "Run as fast as you can." The circumstances weren't as simple. The direction I was to run was straight toward the edge of a cliff, hundreds of feet above town. I had a parachute attached to my back and, supposedly, the wind would pick it up and lift me off the ground before I got to the edge of the cliff.

My heart pounded in fear as I started to run. The drag of the parachute hampered my speed, giving me unwanted extra time to contemplate my fate. The edge of the cliff came closer and closer and then, suddenly, magnificently, I was airborne! The cliff fell away below me, and my fear was replaced by incredible exultation. *I did it!* I was soaring!

Later, safe on the ground, I thought about that experience in regard to my life. There have been many times when a terrifying cliff of circumstances has risen up in my pathway. Looking around desperately, I hear the Holy Spirit whisper, "Run as fast as you can—we're in this together."

And so I start to run, eyes clenched in fear. All of a sudden I feel myself being lifted up by the Spirit, and we begin to soar over the very circumstance I'd thought I couldn't bear. Oh, the wonder of what happens, when against every human instinct, we trust the Holy Spirit's urging to follow Him. We are never alone, and as Christ-followers we can depend on Him any time we face the cliff's edge.

Prayer

    Father, I ask that from your glorious, unlimited resources you will empower me with inner strength through your Spirit, so that Christ will make His home in my heart as I trust in Him. Let my roots grow down into your love and keep me strong. May I have the power to understand how wide, how long, how high, and how deep your love is (Ephesians 3:16-18, page 896).

The most complete description of the work of the Holy Spirit is given in John 14–16 (pages 823-825). These three chapters tell us some of the last things Jesus shared with His disciples before He left them. The most important thing He told them is that they would not be left alone. God would send the Holy Spirit to make His home inside them, to comfort them and remind them of all they'd been taught. The picture Jesus paints of the Holy Spirit is one of tender intimacy, an intimacy that is available to us today.

So far we have learned that the Holy Spirit, Jesus the Son, and God the Father are one Being, sharing the same attributes, which are unique to them. We've learned that it's the Holy Spirit who makes people aware of their sin and is involved in their spiritual birth.

When we receive Jesus Christ as our Savior, we are immediately given the assurance of life with God, life that will never end or be taken away. All believers are sealed with the Holy Spirit, who is God's mark of ownership. This is God's guarantee of our salvation—which does not depend on our living a good life, but on the fact that Jesus died for our sins in our place. As believers, we are assured of entrance into heaven when we die.

Now we're going to see just how personal the Holy Spirit is as He lives in us and enables us to live an abundant life in Christ.

The Holy Spirit's Continued Work in Our Lives

As followers of Jesus Christ, we are not enslaved by our sinful nature. Through the Holy Spirit, we have been born anew and we have access to new resources that enable us to live a godly life. He gives us power to overcome sinful attitudes and habits that prevent us from being what we were designed to be. He helps us understand the Bible and teaches us how to pray.

> *Sinful nature* refers to the sin influence that remains with us after God's new creation has come and we have been born again through the Holy Spirit. Many Bible translations use the term *flesh* instead of *sinful nature*. Galatians 5:16-17 (page 893) tells us that the sinful nature and the Holy Spirit in us are always opposed to each other.

The Christian life is one of continual growth, beginning at the very moment we commit our life to Christ. The Holy Spirit enters our heart, and we begin to discover the incredible level of life God has planned for us. That is not to say life is perfect and without trials from that point on. It doesn't mean we'll never again make self-destructive choices. But it *does* mean that God's Spirit is now living in us, always available and ready, always guiding us to live for Him.

Let's look at some of the ways the Holy Spirit helps us grow as Christ-followers. Read the following verses, and note what they say.

Read 1 John 2:27 (page 942).

What stands out most in this verse?

I love the word "everything." The Holy Spirit will teach us *everything* we need to know. Don't you find that extremely encouraging? How has the Spirit taught you things in your life?

Read Romans 8:14 (page 862).

What does this verse tell us about our relationship with God?

The Message paraphrase of this verse focuses on our opportunities as God's children. "*God's Spirit beckons. There are things to do and places to go!*" Isn't that great? Truly, the Holy Spirit is eager to show us the things God has for us to do and the places for us to go.

Read Galatians 5:22-23 (page 893).

Just imagine if your first reaction to all the daily irritants in your life was patience or gentleness. Imagine going through each day with an innate sense of joy! The more control we give the Spirit over our lives, the more evident these attitudes will be.

Read 2 Corinthians 3:18 (page 883).

What are we changed into?

It's wonderful to think that as we walk with God and listen to the Holy Spirit's prompting within us, we can become a more accurate reflection of Jesus to the world around us.

What do you think about that?

Read Acts 1:8 (page 830).

God has given us His Spirit so that we will have the power and the words to tell others about Him—including our family and friends! Remember, as you relate to those around you, relax, focus on God, and remember that the Holy Spirit is in you. You have His power! Sharing Christ with our family and friends is such an important aspect of our relationship with God. Take some time right now and ask God to set you apart and empower you to be His witness. Write out your prayer.

Reading God's Word

We learned that the Holy Spirit inspired people to write down God's words in the Scriptures. So reading the Bible on a regular basis is an essential part of our understanding of and relationship with God. The Bible is His direct communication to us and the source of answers to life. Note what the following verses say about the Bible.

Psalm 119:105 (page 470)

Did you notice the double reference here? It is both a lamp and a light. That's twice the illumination! God obviously doesn't want us to get lost, and His Word protects us from that.

Read 2 Timothy 3:16-17 (page 915)

What's the very first thing these verses say?

List the ways the Bible is useful to us.

Do you see how God helps us through the Bible in all aspects of our lives? In which area of your life have you seen the Bible challenge and change you the most?

Read Romans 15:4 (page 868).

Do you ever feel like it's taking God a long time to fulfill one of His promises to you? The more you read God's Word, the more hope you'll feel and the more encouragement you'll have. The Bible keeps your focus on God, not on what may seem to you like lack of progress in regard to a particular prayer.

Prayer

Have you ever wondered what Jesus' prayer life was like while He was on earth? We get a glimpse of it in Mark 1:35 (page 762).

What did Jesus do, and when did He do it?

What is the significance of Jesus going to an isolated place before daybreak to pray?

Living on this earth, with all the limitations of a human body, Jesus knew that His strength to show people who God was—and to endure their doubt and rejection—was related to spending time with His Father. It's the same for us. A vibrant prayer life is essential to our relationship with God. It's the means by which we emotionally connect with Him. What do you find the biggest challenge to connecting with God in this way?

What are some ways you can resolve this challenge?

If the solution seems difficult, tell God! Ask Him to help you cultivate the kind of prayer life He wants you to have. Remember, the Holy Spirit is your personal Advocate. He has a major role in the vital matter of prayer. It's something you'll be very excited about!

Read Romans 8:26-27 (pages 862-863).

The Holy Spirit helps us in our weakness! Have you ever been in such distress you don't even know how to put your heartache into words? *You don't have to know!* What does this passage say?

Weakness can mean many things. Read Romans 8:23 to find out more.

What kind of weakness is described? Is it just the kind of weakness we experience once in a while, or when we have done our best and can't do any more? Or is it something all-encompassing?

Our bodies will never be free of sin and suffering in this life. There is never a time here on earth when we do not experience this kind of weakness.

What does this mean in regard to the help of the Holy Spirit when we pray?

Yes! Our Advocate, the One who pleads our case for us in all matters, *always* helps us. We should still pray—in those everyday times, in those desperate times when we don't have the words. It gives us comfort to know that God has provided the Holy Spirit to always be there as we pray.

The Spirit always pleads for us in harmony with God's will for us. What does Romans 8:28-29 (page 863) say the result of our prayers and the pleading of the Spirit will be?

God created us to be in relationship with Him. He communicates to us through the Bible, and we communicate with Him through prayer conversations and worship. Don't allow yourself to be robbed of this vital aspect of your relationship with God. God Himself, the Holy Spirit, is helping you!

What does 1 Thessalonians 5:17 (page 907) tell us to do?

What does it mean to "never stop praying"?

Have you had the experience of either talking to someone or doing something, but at the exact same time you were praying? How did that help you?

Jesus also spoke about prayer, in Matthew 6:5-6 (page 737). What does He say?

Let's read a couple more verses about prayer before we move on. Turn to 1 John 5:14-15 (pages 943-944).

What does the beginning phrase say?

We can be 100 percent confident that God hears our prayer! Isn't that wonderful?

There is a caution, though. What is it?

Think about this for a moment. What kind of prayers would not please God?

Think over some past conversations you've had. Have there been some you've found particularly tiresome? The most tiresome conversations are usually with very self-involved people, where all you do is nod your head occasionally. On the other hand, have you had a conversation where it felt more like communion—where you were completely in tune with what the other was saying, and every word was pure pleasure? Those are the kind of prayers that please God—not the self-involved, "gimme, gimme!" ones. God's desire is for us to hear *His* heart as He hears ours.

It's interesting to note that in the example of prayer Jesus shared with His disciples when they asked Him to teach them how to pray, there are no singular pronouns except the ones referring to God! (Matthew 6:9-13, page 737). The pronouns referring to people are all plural, so you are praying for and with others as you pray for yourself.

True prayer comes from our hearts. It originates in the heart of God, who communicates it to us through His Holy Spirit. And the Spirit in turn helps us communicate with the Father.

Obedience

God's life is in us through the Holy Spirit. We now have a desire
to listen to the Spirit and understand God's Word. So it is not
enough to just read the Bible. We should determine to do what
it says.

Read James 1:22-25 (page 930). What does it say?

If we only read the words on the page, what are we doing?

If we put what we read into practice, what will happen?

Foolishness or blessing. When you look at it like that, the choice
is obvious, isn't it? God's blessings are incomparable!

The truth of the matter is, as long as we live on this earth, there
will always be a struggle between our flesh and our spirit. Read Galatians 5:17 (page 893).

In what ways do you identify with this verse?

This is why the Holy Spirit is such a precious gift to us. He is always drawing us toward God. He is always empowering us to make the right choice. The more we read the Bible and the more time we spend in prayer, the easier it is to respond to His promptings.

The fact is that we cannot obey God's will independently of the Holy Spirit. We need His life to give us the strength and ability to do it! There is a wonderful verse to keep in mind. In fact, it is an important verse to memorize. Read 1 Corinthians 10:13 (page 876).

Isn't it nice to know you are not alone in your struggles to live the new way? We're all in the same boat here. But what does it say after that?

Those are beautiful words, aren't they? Write them down and then just stop for a minute and meditate on that wonderful truth. *God is faithful!*

Now before we look at the next part of this verse, let's decide to be honest, okay? God says He will not allow you to be tempted beyond what you can stand. He also says He will show you a way out. Remember, we're all in the same boat here. And we've all given in to temptations—both big and little—which means we all missed the exit sign that God had flashing for us.

Think of a time you made the wrong choice. What was going on at the time? Were you overtired, overbusy? Were you feeling disconnected from God and neglecting time for prayer and Bible reading? Looking back, can you recognize the exact moment in which you could have escaped the temptation?

It's very important to be able to answer these questions, so you can avoid drifting away from closeness with God and making the same mistake again. If you're not sure, ask God to show you the answers. Nine times out of ten the inability to fight off temptation is the result of becoming disconnected in your relationship with God, which leads to ambivalence toward the Bible and prayer.

God has taken up residence inside you. Isn't that wonderful to think about? And having the Holy Spirit within you marks you as belonging to God!

Read 1 Corinthians 6:19-20 (page 873).

What must we realize?

Yes! Here is an answer to those times of thinking we're distant from God, which lead to giving in to temptation. We must realize that the Holy Spirit lives in us. We *are* close to God, and we belong to Him, the One who loves us. How does understanding and believing these things help you stay away from sin?

There is more about our ongoing struggle with temptation in Galatians 5:16 (page 893). What does it say?

How can you let the Holy Spirit guide your life?

The Holy Spirit will be faithful in helping us grow as we listen to God and obey Him. Each morning, we can pray about our activities, asking God to reveal His plans for our day. We can ask Him to give us the wisdom we need to accomplish things His way. As we live aware of the presence of the Holy Spirit in us moment by moment, our life will reveal a whole new meaning and purpose. Each day we will see evidence of God working in us.

——— *Personal Reflection and Application* ———

From this chapter,

I see...

I believe…

I will…

Prayer

Father, help me to pay attention to what you say. Let me listen carefully to your words. Don't let me lose sight of them. Let them penetrate deep into my heart, so they will bring life to me and health to my whole body (Proverbs 4:20-22, page 483).

Thoughts, Notes, and Prayer Requests

_____

_____

_____

_____

_____

_____

_____

_____

_____

_____

What Does the Holy Spirit Bring to My Life?

My aunt was teaching me how to crochet. Never one to discourage, she didn't even bat an eye when I showed her what I wanted to make—a 72-inch-round pineapple-pattern tablecloth. None of those silly little washcloths everyone else starts out with for me!

My aunt was a good teacher, and in no time at all, my tablecloth was about 20 inches across. The center was done, and I was starting on the pineapple pattern. *This was fun!* The only part I didn't like was when my aunt took my crocheting from my hand to examine my work. Sometimes she nodded in approval. Sometimes—more often than I thought was merited—she'd frown and start unraveling my work to reveal a mistake.

My tablecloth had reached about 65 inches across when she again asked to see my work. I reluctantly handed it over. Several rows back I'd made a mistake, and I didn't want her to find it. *I was so close to being done!* I watched in dread as she examined my work. Eventually she got around to my mistake. Frowning, she bent her head down for a closer look. Then she glanced up at me. I glanced down at my fingernails.

"You can't let that mistake stay," she said. "Even if no one else sees it, you and I both know it's there." And with that she started pulling on the thread—and pulling and pulling—unraveling hours and hours and *hours* of work in about five minutes. I wanted to scream, "Stop! I can live with it." I wanted to cry. I even wanted to get angry with her—but I knew she was right. The tablecloth would not be the tablecloth of my dreams if I left the mistake intact.

Prayer

Lord, give me complete knowledge of your will and spiritual wisdom and understanding, so that the way I live will always honor and please you, and my life will produce every kind of good fruit (Colossians 1:9-10a, page 902).

God's plan for us is a full and satisfying life characterized by inner peace and joy. He wants us to live moment by moment under the direction of His Holy Spirit. The moment we are saved, God gifts us with the Holy Spirit, who is continually with us, leading us and guiding us. Many Christians do not live the full life God wants for them because they keep trying to live life on their own terms. They try to live independently of God, using the strength of the flesh and making concessions for their wrong choices, just as I tried to make a concession for the mistake in my tablecloth. I'm so glad that my aunt insisted on excellence because now when I look at my handiwork, I feel no shame, only satisfaction in a job well done. God wants us to experience the abundance and excellence that comes from living life on His terms, under the control of the Holy Spirit. This kind of life produces wonderful fruit, which is what we're talking about in this chapter.

In chapter 3, we learned that the Holy Spirit plays an active role in our Christian growth. He transforms us to be more and more like Jesus. As our Advocate and Helper, He is making it possible for us to pray as we need to, to understand the Bible, and to obey what we read. In this chapter, we're going to see the results of living according to the Holy Spirit's guidance.

Fruit of the Spirit

Read Galatians 5:22-23 (page 893) and list the nine qualities that are the natural product of the Holy Spirit in our lives.

1.

2.

3.

4.

5.

6.

7.

8.

9.

These are inner qualities, which we all want to possess, but they are not *natural* human qualities. They are produced only by God's indwelling Spirit. They're the outward expression of our inner life. These are not separate qualities that can be divided. A close look at this passage of Scripture indicates they are a unit. God desires that we would display all of them, not just one or two.

Bible teacher J. Sidlow Baxter notes that the way the characteristics of the fruit are listed, they fall into three groups: attitude, action, and application. The first three fruits are love, joy, and peace; these are inward attitudes. The next three are patience, kindness, and goodness; these are outward actions toward others. The last three are faithfulness, gentleness, and self-control; these are upward applications. They are the first essentials of godliness. When you look at the fruit of the Spirit in this way, you realize it encompasses all the relationships of life.[1] Let's look at each aspect of the fruit separately.

Love

It's no surprise love is listed first. According to 1 Corinthians 13:13 (page 878), it is the greatest quality. God Himself is love, so love must be reflected in all of our relationships. Read the following verses and note the relationship it talks about next to the reference.

Matthew 22:34-40 (page 753)

Titus 2:3-4 (page 917)

Colossians 3:19 (page 904)

John 13:34-35 (page 823)

Luke 6:27-28 (page 786)

Now why did God have to include our enemies on the list? The answer is simple. God Himself is love, so He loves His enemies. He loved us when we were His enemies, before we were saved through Jesus. Now He lives in us in the Person of His Holy Spirit, who empowers us to have love as the motivation behind everything we do—including interactions with our enemies. This is a big part of the life of joy and peace He wants for us. When love is the governor of our attitude, the negative relationships in our lives lose the power they hold over us. Love frees us, it empowers us, and it puts everything in right perspective.

Read Ephesians 5:1-2 (page 897).

Do you see what I mean by right perspective? Think of the person you have the most difficult relationship with—or that you consider an enemy. When you line your feelings up with that verse, what conclusion do you arrive at?

Take a moment and be honest with God. He already knows how you feel about this person. He already knows the control this person has over your life because of those feelings. Tell Him you want to do what He does because you are His dear child, but you need His help. God is love and He will help you!

Love could actually be included in each of the three groups because it's not only an attitude, but it's also an action and an application. Love isn't just an emotion. It's also an action based in the determination of our will, as we respond to what God has done for us. First John 4:19 (page 943) says, *"We love each other because he loved us first."*

Read Romans 12:9-10 (page 866). List the five directives.

God just can't stop talking about love, can He? In *The Message*, the last command is paraphrased, "*practice playing second fiddle*." And that's what love involves—sacrificing yourself. And while an attitude of love might seem daunting in regard to some people in your life, remember, we're not trying to do this alone.

Read Romans 5:5 (page 860).

God fills our hearts with *His* love through the Holy Spirit. His love in us makes things possible that are completely impossible without Him.

Joy

Joy is more than happiness. Happiness is dependent on our circumstances. Joy is not. Our relationship with God is both the foundation and source of our joy. It's always with us, regardless of our circumstances.

Read Psalm 43:3-4 (page 433). What—or who—is the source of the psalmist's joy?

What does Philippians 4:4 (page 901) say about when and in whom we should have joy?

James 1:2 (page 930) says, "*When troubles come your way, consider it an opportunity for great joy.*" This shows that joy is an attitude determined through our will, rather than an emotional response. At first, it's hard to separate joy from happiness because we are so used to considering it an emotion. But when you remember that God is the source of your joy, and that He has made His home in you through the Holy Spirit, it's easier to see it as an attitude. You feel deep joy knowing your difficult circumstance is in the hands of God, who loves you immeasurably.

Looking at it in this way, can you think of a time when you felt joy during a distressing time?

Peace

Peace is a tranquility that floods your heart and spirit and keeps you in harmony with God.

What does Philippians 4:6-7 (page 901) say about peace?

What does God's peace do?

Worry and peace are mutually exclusive. You cannot worry and have peace. It's impossible. Peace, like love and joy, is an attitude that naturally comes through the Holy Spirit as you determine by your will to follow His lead, regardless of your circumstance.

Along with prayer, what else is mentioned in verse 6 that is necessary before experiencing God's peace?

An attitude of thankfulness builds an attitude of peace. If, every time you start to worry, you replace that thought with one of thankfulness, worry will lose its grip and peace will pervade your spirit.

Now turn to John 14:27 (page 824).

Is there any way to experience this peace if you are not under the control of God's Spirit?

What circumstance is causing you to worry and is robbing you of God's gift of peace? Write out a prayer that replaces your worry with thankfulness.

Now take a moment and let God's gift of peace wash over you.

The next category of fruit represents action that focuses outward.

Patience

Read Romans 15:4-5 (page 868).

What is it that we need patience for?

Where does patience come from?

Have you thought of that before—that *you* don't develop patience—God *gives* it to you? Does that give you hope about experiencing patience in your life?

What's a current situation in your life where you really need some patience?

Now, realizing the source of your needed patience is God and not you, how does that make a difference in the situation?

It is the Holy Spirit who gives you all the patience you need. You just have to depend on Him.

Kindness

Kindness means thoughtful consideration—courteous and kindly action. Read Colossians 3:12-13 (pages 903-904).

What are we reminded of in the first phrase?

What three things are we told to do because of who we are?

Read this passage again. What is the little four-letter word preceding the first directive?

Must—that doesn't leave any room, does it? When we know that we're loved and chosen by God to be holy, does it make sense to do anything else besides what these directives tell us? And the word *clothe* could be substituted for *cover*, so this isn't a partial or temporary action. It's an action that defines us. What are some ways that you have shown kindness in the past, or new ways that you can choose to show kindness in the future?

Goodness

Goodness is the total of all God's attributes, revealing His all-encompassing love, incomparable righteousness, holiness, and perfect divine character. What does Ephesians 2:10 (page 896) say?

I find this verse completely overwhelming. God considers us His *masterpiece!*

When you look at yourself in the mirror, do you see a masterpiece? God does! He loves the result of His creativity that is you. He loves the image you are reflecting of His Son, and He anticipates what will come from you doing the good things He has planned for you to do.

Now we come to the last category of fruit, which focuses upward as it is displayed in our lives.

Faithfulness

Faith signifies confidence in God. Our faithfulness indicates God's presence in our life and displays Him—and us—as someone trustworthy and reliable. Read Luke 16:10-12 (pages 798-799).

What, in particular, strikes you in these verses?

Did you get the implication that faithfulness is an all-pervasive quality, involving both the insignificant and significant aspects of our life? Our faithfulness in all matters displays to the world one of the most outstanding qualities of God—that He, and thus we as His representatives, can be trusted in all things.

Gentleness

Gentleness is a character trait Jesus exhibited repeatedly during His earthly life. We see His gentleness in action when a group of self-righteous religious leaders are ready to stone to death a woman who'd been caught in the act of adultery. They dragged her to the temple and stood her in front of Jesus, demanding He make a statement.

Can you imagine the emotional tangle of that moment—the angry men, the terrified, humiliated woman, the tense crowd waiting to see what would happen? But Jesus refused to be caught up in the emotion. His response to both the woman and her accusers was immensely gentle. No accusations, no attitude of judgment—even though there was room for both—just pure gentleness expressing absolute truth (John 8:1-11, pages 816-817).

Read Matthew 11:28-30 (page 742).

How does Jesus describe Himself in verse 29?

That's what He wants us to learn from Him. And remember, we have the Holy Spirit inside us, the one who is reminding us of everything Jesus told us. Jesus set the example of how to respond to people and circumstances. If we allow the Spirit to control us, what will the result be?

Self-Control

Self-control is one aspect of the fruit that comes from being under the control of the Holy Spirit. Read Galations 5:22-25 (page 893).

What do verses 24 and 25 remind us of?

Isn't that great? Because of what God has done, we do not have to yield to sinful passions and desires. We have power through

His Spirit to live a life of love, joy, peace, patience—all of these—and self-control.

When you lose control, what usually results?

Self-control solves problems; lack of self-control creates problems. The Holy Spirit in our lives is always a problem-solver, and we can maintain self-control only under His control.

Author Elizabeth George says, "Throughout the Bible, the word *fruit* refers to what is within. If what is inside a person is good, the fruit of that person's life will be good. If what is inside is rotten, the fruit of that person's life will also be bad."[2] As we continue to walk in the Spirit and become more like Jesus, our lives will bring glory and praise to God.

Gifts of the Spirit

Gifts of the Spirit are different than the *fruit* of the Spirit. *All* Christians receive *all* aspects of the fruit of the Spirit because they receive the Spirit Himself. However, the *gifts* of the Spirit are different. All believers receive at least *one* gift when they accept Jesus as their Savior. Read 1 Corinthians 12:11 (page 877).

Now go back a few verses to 1 Corinthians 12:7. Also read 1 Peter 4:10 (page 936). What are we to use our gifts for?

Do you see the difference between the fruit of the Spirit and the gifts of the Spirit? The *fruit* of the Spirit shows who God is inside us. He is loving, joyful, peaceful, patient, kind, good, faithful, gentle, and self-controlled. The fruit enriches our relationship with God Himself and with others. The *gifts* of the Spirit are to be used in serving others, which brings glory to God. Bible teacher Charles Ryrie distinguishes between natural abilities, learned skills, and spiritual gifts. Natural abilities are health, IQ, mechanical aptitude, and so forth. Learned skills include things like culinary abilities, carpentry, working with computers, good writing or speaking, and so on. Spiritual gifts are gifts to be used in serving others, by which we ultimately serve the Lord.[3]

Read Ephesians 4:11-12 (page 897), which lists some of the gifts. What kind of service is emphasized?

Read 1 Corinthians 12:8-10 (page 877) and Romans 12:6-8 (page 866). List the gifts of the Spirit included here and in Ephesians 4:11.

The Holy Spirit gives us the gift or gifts that fit the plan God has for our lives. As we obey His Word and allow ourselves to be led by the Spirit each day, we'll automatically be using our gift or gifts without even knowing it. Many times, we discover what gift or gifts we have because the Holy Spirit has made us so effective in that special ministry. We also realize how natural it is and how much we enjoy serving in that capacity. It's wonderful to contemplate how thoroughly God has equipped and gifted us according to His unique plan for us!

In what ways do you see this in your life?

Personal Reflection and Application

From this chapter,

I see…

I believe…

I will…

Prayer

Father, help me to grow as I learn to know you better and better. Help me to be strengthened with all your glorious power, so I will have all the endurance and patience I need. Fill me with joy as I walk with you (Colossians 1:10b-11, page 902).

Thoughts, Notes, and Prayer Requests

Living in the Power
of the Holy Spirit

Chuck Swindoll, pastor and author, tells the following story:

A young man named Sinner received the gift of a beautiful new red car from his Father. Its name was Salvation, and it was brand-new and spanking clean. The young man was so delighted by his gift that he talked about it all the time, telling everyone it was a gift from his Father. He never could have afforded such a car, but he hadn't had to pay a cent. It was a free gift!

The car made him so happy that he changed his name from Sinner to Saved. Time passed, and one day he was seen pushing his car down the highway. A man named Helper walked up, introduced Himself, and offered to help.

"No, thanks. I'm doing fine," Saved answered.

"Have you pushed your car very far?" Helper asked.

"About 200 miles. It's been hard, but it's the least I can do for my Father, who gave it to me."

"Please allow me to help you," Helper said. "There's something you don't understand."

Helper opened the door on the passenger side, inviting the young man to seat himself. He hesitated, but thought it was worth a try and climbed in. For the first time since he'd received the car, he started to relax.

Helper walked around and got into the driver's seat. He started the motor, and soon they were traveling down the highway quietly and smoothly. It was exhilarating!

The young man sat there amazed. He was allowing the Helper to do what he couldn't do. He'd thought reaching the end of the road was his responsibility. He smiled with relief and suddenly realized that it was the first time he'd smiled since he'd received his gift.[4]

Prayer

Father, the Creator of everything in heaven and on earth, I pray that from your glorious, unlimited resources you will empower me with inner strength through your Spirit, so that Christ will make His home in my heart as I trust. Let my roots grow down into your love and keep me strong (Ephesians 3:14-17, page 896).

Chuck Swindoll concludes the above story by saying, "The one who gave you the car also gave you the driver. He can handle it. When you try to wrestle the wheel from His hand, you have terrible wrecks."

This is a picture of how many Christians are living. We understand that there was no way we could have ever paid for our salvation. It was a gift. However, we don't know that the power to *live* the Christian life is a gift too. The presence of the Holy Spirit in our lives and the gifts He brings with Him allow us to live a Christlike life. For believers, the Holy Spirit is always there, always reminding us that we are God's children as He guides us, teaches us, and gives us the power to live above our circumstances.

Let's review some of what we've learned so far. Our salvation is a free gift to us provided by Jesus' death on the cross. Read Romans 5:8-11 (page 860).

What is the natural reaction to having a relationship with God through Jesus?

Jesus' death made our salvation possible, and His resurrection provides us with new life—His life—through the Holy Spirit living within us. Sometimes it is still difficult to accept that we can do nothing to make our salvation more secure than the day we accepted Jesus as our Savior. But the Spirit in us is our guarantee from God that He will carry through what He has begun!

If that's not encouraging enough, read Ephesians 1:18-20 (page 895).

What is the first thing Paul says?

There are two powerful phrases in that first verse: "*flooded with light*" and "*confident hope.*" Sometimes when our circumstances are "flooded with light," the last thing we feel is hope because the reality—all the impossibilities and challenges—are fully illuminated. But this verse says that when our hearts are flooded with light in regard to God, we will have not just hope, but we will have *confident hope*.

We will see the reality of who God is and how utterly trustworthy He is—not to mention that He sees us as His *rich and glorious inheritance*.

What is the second thing Paul says?

Don't rush through this part because it is truly amazing. When we believe in God, we have access to the incredible greatness of His power—the very same power that raised Jesus from the dead. Think about that! Are you starting to comprehend the greatness of the power God has made available to you?

What do you think stands in your way?

Our day-to-day, moment-by-moment progress is provided by Christ's resurrection power. It's by God's power, not our own power, that we remain close to Him and obey His will. We can't do it by ourselves. Trying to is like pushing the car (with the brakes on too)!

Being Filled with the Spirit

What does it mean to be *filled* with the Spirit? You might be thinking, "I thought I received all of the Spirit when I became a Christian." Don't worry; you did! To be filled with the Spirit doesn't mean we need to acquire something we don't already have. It means to allow ourselves to be constantly yielded to the Holy Spirit's control. We say "yes" to Him moment by moment. To do this, we have to give up the desire to control our own lives. In other words, we climb into the passenger seat and enjoy the view of wherever the Holy Spirit leads us.

Read Ephesians 5:18-20 (page 898).

Why do you suppose being filled with God's Spirit is compared with drunkenness?

When someone is drunk with alcohol, they are under the influence and power of the alcohol they have consumed. In the same way, a Christian who is filled with God's Holy Spirit is under the influence and power of God.

How will a person who is filled with the Holy Spirit act?

It paints a pretty joyful picture, doesn't it? Singing, making music, giving thanks for everything. *That's exactly what God intends!*

God commands us to be filled with His Spirit for two reasons: to bring us to maturity and to serve Him in special ways. We are given the Holy Spirit at the moment of our new birth, but we are not spiritually mature at that point. Maturity comes with time and experience.

With each obedient step, we gain experience in how faithful and trust-worthy God is. That, in turn, gives us confidence to be more obedient and follow Him more closely.

Sometimes our maturity is slow in coming. Such was the case with the Christians of Corinth, who we read about in 1 Corinthians 3:1-3 (page 871).

What did Paul have to feed them with since they were not spiritually mature?

What were the Christians being controlled by?

When we refuse to access the power that is ours through the Holy Spirit, we live under the control of the sinful nature, or the flesh. We live as though we didn't know God. What a limited, diminished life! It's not the life of joy and power and closeness that God desires.

Letting God Transform Us

The work God does in our life when we surrender our own way and believe in Him for salvation takes us from darkness to light (Ephesians 5:8-9, page 897). This attitude of surrender needs to be an ongoing action so that God will keep enriching our lives and bringing us to maturity. Read Romans 12:2 (page 866).

What will God do when we allow Him to transform us?

God will *change the way we think* (don't you love that?) as we let Him transform us! Read Romans 8:5 (page 862).

What is the pattern that is described here?

Who or what we are controlled by determines how we think, and the way we think determines the way we behave. When we let God transform us and our thought pattern changes, our behavior changes. As a result of our internal change, it becomes easier to surrender to God's transformation process. It's when we compromise that our walk becomes difficult—trying to follow Him on our own, independent terms. It doesn't work. It keeps us immature, quarreling, and jealous.

> The cost is surrender. The condition is obedience. When the Holy Spirit entered my life, I received all of Him. If I am to be filled with His Spirit, He needs all of me.

Is there an area of your life where you know your thinking and behavior need to change?

Take some time right now and ask God to help you be willing to let Him transform this area of your life.

Let's stop for a moment and do a quick self-evaluation. On the left side of the page is a list of things that are evidence of a Spirit-filled life. If you feel you are lacking in any area, on the right side make note of it and what changes you want to see happen.

Evidence of being filled with God's Spirit:	What I plan to do where change is needed:
Knowing I am saved	
Praying regularly	
Reading and meditating on God's Word, the Bible	
Being controlled by the Spirit, not sinful habits	
Loving other believers	
Having concern for unbelievers	

It is impossible to live in obedience to God if we live by the sinful nature. That's why God gave us His Holy Spirit—so we could live in Him and in His strength.

──────── *Personal Reflection and Application* ────────

From this chapter,

I see...

I believe...

I will...

∽

Prayer

Father, help me to surrender my body to you because of all you have done for me. Let me be a living and holy sacrifice—the kind you will find acceptable. I know this is truly the way to worship you. Help me not to copy the behavior and customs of this world but to let you transform me into a new person by changing the way I think. Then I will learn to know your will for me, which is good and pleasing and perfect (Romans 12:1-2, page 866).

──────── *Thoughts, Notes, and Prayer Requests* ────────

_____

_____

_____

6

Enjoying the Presence
of the Holy Spirit

The midnight sky was dark and stormy as I drove the winding mountain road toward home. My two boys were asleep in the backseat, and I used the quiet time to mull over the situation we were facing. With my husband out of work, bills were stacking up and tensions were mounting.

Suddenly there was a loud "thunk," and the car slowed to a stop. I sat in black silence, not sure what to do. Inexplicably, I felt no fear. I knew I wasn't alone.

Far back in the trees a faint light gleamed. I shook my little guys awake, and we trudged through the dark woods. "God is taking us on an adventure!" I told them.

The light belonged to a house, and though I hated knocking so late on a strange door, an uncanny confidence filled me. "Come in, come in!" said a cheerful little man. "What brings you out on such a night?" I told him my plight. "Let me make a quick phone call," he said.

The next thing I knew we were bundled into his car and driven a few miles down the road to a fishing lodge, where he handed us off to the elderly proprietor. She showed us to a room where a fire was laid and the bedding turned back—as if we were expected. I turned to her, knowing I couldn't afford it, but before I said a word she smiled and said, "I don't take money from stranded women. Sleep well."

I tucked the boys into their beds and climbed into mine, marveling at this unexpected treat, compliments of God. I'd not felt one moment of fear—His Spirit had reassured me every moment that we were, indeed, on an adventure.

Prayer

Father, thank you for giving me your Spirit to dwell in me and be my Guide and Teacher of truth. Help me to better grasp what it means to know His presence (John 14:16-17, page 823).

There is often a striking outward difference between someone who knows God and someone who is just a good person. It's a difference that's sometimes hard to put your finger on, because there are many good people in this world—honest, hardworking people—making a worthy contribution to life. But people who live their lives under the control of the Holy Spirit are in a different realm. As every part of their life is impacted by the Holy Spirit's control, that in turn impacts the people they come in contact with.

Although everyone who has a relationship with Jesus has the possibility of being that kind of different, many Christians choose to keep their distance from God. They try to live independently of the Holy Spirit living within them. And let's be honest. When we consider all the fruit that should be evident in our lives and all the other attributes we've been reading about, it does seem impossible to consistently stay so intimate with God.

Think of a time when you thought this type of life was too difficult. What was it that got you through that experience?

Are you perhaps now feeling that this kind of Christian life is too difficult?

Those times come when we're behind our little red car...pushing, pushing, pushing...rather than resting in the passenger seat and allowing the Holy Spirit to take us where He wants. The fact is that the life God wants us to have is absolutely impossible without the Spirit. Are we going to insist on remaining alone and toughing it out on our own? Or are we going to throw in the towel on our own efforts, turn to the Spirit, and depend on His energy?

Remaining in Him

In John 15:1-8 (page 824) there is a vivid picture of how we can accomplish the impossible—through the Holy Spirit within us.

Who does the grapevine represent?

Who does the gardener represent?

Who does the branch represent?

Go back over the passage and circle the word *remain*. How many times does that word appear? That obviously means the concept of *remaining* is extremely significant to what Jesus is saying here. What is the significance of that word in this context?

Merriam-Webster's Collegiate Dictionary defines *remain* as "to continue unchanged." Our vibrant, fruit-bearing life will continue unchanged only as long as we stay connected to Jesus.

How much can we do apart from Jesus?

The life-giving Holy Spirit is inside us to keep us connected to and at home in Christ, who infuses us with His power, His peace, His joy, and His energy. The natural result is fruit.

Who is doing the pruning?

Yes! God the Father is. He's the gardener. There is absolutely no struggle on our part to bear fruit—we simply have to stay attached to Christ and fruit will develop.

What does the gardener do to the branches that are bearing fruit?

The Father's desire is for us to bear much fruit. The pruning we experience is not to punish us but to enable us to bear even more fruit.

Is there an area of your life that you feel God the Father has been pruning? What has been the result?

Pruning could be a terrifying, destructive process if it weren't the Father who was doing it. Thankfully, that is not the case. He knows completely what He is doing. And He knows us and loves us completely. We can trust Him with the areas of our life He prunes. He will not injure or destroy us—He will multiply us.

Remain is also translated *abide*. This word can sound old-fashioned, but it can help us better understand. Abide also means "to stay" or "to remain," but in the sense of living somewhere or making your home there. Doesn't that make the picture more beautiful?

Take a moment now and tell God you trust Him. Write out the words if you'd like. Let Him know that even though you sometimes feel afraid, you want to fully remain in Him and receive His tender care.

Since *remaining* is key to bearing fruit, what are some ways we can remain in God?

Anything that helps us maintain an intimate relationship with God will assure that we "remain." We remain connected to the vine through prayer and Bible study. We remain connected through our obedience. All of these things keep us listening to God and staying close to Him.

The closer we grow to Him, the better we will know Him and trust Him and the more our faith will grow. The way to know God is to trust Him and become familiar with the Bible.

Listening to God the Father speak through His Word and the Holy Spirit is a sure way to remain in Him. Just as being connected to the vine means life to the branches, being connected to Jesus means a spiritual, fruitful life for us. All three Persons of the Trinity work together to keep us productive!

Refusing to Let the Holy Spirit Work in Us

In what ways can we refuse to allow the Holy Spirit to do His work? Let's find out.

Read Acts 7:51-54 (page 836), in which a believer named Stephen is speaking, and note what it says.

Who is Stephen speaking to, and how are his hearers reacting?

Stubborn resistance and unbelief will keep people from receiving salvation. They refuse to listen when the Holy Spirit is convicting them of sin.

Read 1 Thessalonians 5:19-22 (page 907) and note what it says.

Do you see any of these tendencies in yourself? Personally, I know that I have stifled the Holy Spirit at times. I have felt His clear prompting to speak to someone or do something, but then I talk myself out of it. Has this happened to you?

How have you stopped yourself from stifling the Holy Spirit in the past?

Read Ephesians 4:30-32 (page 897).

What role of the Spirit is emphasized?

When you ignore the fact that you belong to God, what sort of things result that bring sorrow to the Spirit?

What criteria would you use to assess whether you are living in a way that makes Him glad?

Spiritual Warfare

A Spirit-filled life is powerful, but it is also a life that is tested. Don't be surprised when trials and hardships come your way. Read James 1:2-5 (page 930). What is an opportunity for great joy?

Hmm. Do you consider trouble to be an *opportunity for joy*? It's not the usual attitude, is it? But what does verse 4 say the end result will be?

That is the source of our joy! Even when we're in the middle of devastating circumstances, we can anticipate what the end result will be—we will be perfect and complete, needing nothing—

or as *The Message* paraphrases it, *"mature and well-developed, not deficient in any way."* I like the idea of not being deficient, don't you?

Our Spiritual Armor

There will always be an ongoing struggle between the flesh—the sinful nature—and the Holy Spirit in us, as we learned in Galatians 5:17 (page 893). That's just part of being a Christian, which God fully understands. In the Bible, it likens this struggle to a battle. There is a great passage of Scripture that teaches us how to equip ourselves for it. Read Ephesians 6:10-18 (page 898).

What are the pieces of armor it mentions?

Do you see how protected you are when you make these pieces of armor an integral part of your life? When truth and righteousness are wrapped around you, it is very difficult to be deceived by lies or enticed by unrighteous ploys. When you are walking in the peace that comes from the Good News, you are protected from worry or anxiety. With your faith firmly in front of you, your focus is on God

Woven through all of this armor, standing in front of you, beside you, behind you, above and below you, and especially inside you, is God the Holy Spirit. Not even for a nanosecond are you alone in this battle!

and not your circumstances. And the Word of God keeps all of this active and strong in your life.

There are two other verses worth noting in regard to our armor. Read 2 Corinthians 6:7 (page 885). Where are we to hold these weapons of righteousness?

What is the significance of holding them in our hands?

Read Psalm 50:15 (page 436). This is an interesting verse. It has three parts to it. What are they?

We can call upon God in prayer; prayer is essential to victory. It keeps the Holy Spirit in the driver's seat, and it keeps us yielded to God's will. God does hear our prayers, and He will rescue us when we need to be. But think about that last part: "*You will give me glory.*" "Giving glory" to someone is not something that happens much at all today. Maybe you are puzzled about the phrase. When we speak of giving glory to God, we are giving Him the credit and praising Him for doing something in and through our lives. We give glory to God when we exhibit the reality of His working in our lives day by day.

What will giving God glory look like in your life?

If you think about it, the entire process mentioned in Psalm 50:15 gives God glory. Calling out to God, instead of going it alone, gives God glory. His answer, clear for all to see, gives Him glory. And most amazing of all, when we give Him glory, the whole universe sees something astounding. We—mere humans—have been created with the ability to give Him—the infinite, mighty God—glory. That gives Him even more glory!

Spiritual Growth and Victory

Now that we've seen our armor, let's look at some battle tactics that will bring victory.

The first tactic is to be covered with *every* piece of armor. We've already talked about this, but let's take a deeper look at Ephesians 6:13 (page 898). What does it say?

Yes! To remain standing firm till the end, we need to be fully covered with every piece of armor.

Read 1 Peter 5:8-10 (page 937).

What are the three key thoughts?

Read Ephesians 4:22-27 (page 897). This passage is great because it gets right down to specifics.

How is our sinful nature described in this passage?

Who renews your thoughts and attitudes?

Our new nature has been created to be the same way that God is—truly righteous and holy. That means that our spirits now match up with God the Holy Spirit, whose home is inside us. Amazing!

Are lies and uncontrolled anger compatible with who we are?

Who is given room to work by uncontrolled anger?

Lies we believe about ourselves are just as damaging as lies we tell about or to others. For example, what are some lies you tell yourself that inhibit you from living by the Spirit and fulfilling God's plan? (*I'm too shy...I'm not good enough...I'm not smart enough...*)

What about anger? An attitude of anger blocks the Holy Spirit's input into our lives. It's debilitating to our relationship with Him—and with everyone else. Letting go of justified anger is a particular challenge. Nonetheless, let go of it before the sun goes down, whether you deserve to be angry or not. Choose to let the Spirit, who loves you, control you—instead of anger, which only tears you down.

What anger (or resentment) are you nurturing right now? Take a moment to examine it, and then put your determination to release it and take hold of the Spirit into words. Specify exactly what this emotional release will look like to you.

Read James 4:6-8 (page 932) and note what it says.

Aren't these wonderful verses? First of all, they remind us about God's grace to stand against evil desires. He always gives us *more* grace. Second, they use the word *flee*. If we resist Satan, he's not going to just saunter away—he's going to flee. God can use our obedience in resisting the enemy's taunting and temptation. Third, did you feel an immediate reassurance as you read those words? God's presence is so real when we move toward Him. His desire is that nothing comes between us.

|||||||||||||||||||||||||||||

When we live life aware of God's Spirit in us, when we allow Him to transform us and change our minds to obey Him, life is an adventure that nothing else will ever equal. We never know what a day will bring. But we do know that God loves to lavish His children with blessings they don't expect. God finishes what He starts, and He started a good thing in us. Read Philippians 1:6 (page 899).

God started His work, and He will complete it. But because you are His, something else will happen, and that is our part. Read 2 Peter 3:18 (page 940).

What is our part in God's "good thing"?

What are some practical steps you intend to take to assure your continued growth in the grace and knowledge of our Lord and Savior Jesus Christ?

It has been a great pleasure doing this study together. Its purpose was to deepen our relationship with our infinitely loving and holy God as we become more familiar with the incredible gift of His Holy Spirit He has placed within us. Go in the Spirit's presence and power, and impact your world!

—————— *Personal Reflection and Application* ——————

From this chapter,

I see…

I believe…

I will…

Prayer

Father, thank you that I am led by your Spirit, that you have adopted me as your child, and that I may call you "Dear Father" or "Daddy." I rejoice in the Spirit's affirming that I am your child, an heir together with Christ (Romans 8:14-17, page 862).

─────── *Thoughts, Notes, and Prayer Requests* ───────

Journal Pages

Know God

It does not matter what has happened in your past. No matter what you've done, no matter how you've lived your life,

God is personally interested in you right now.
He cares about you.

God understands your frustration, your loneliness, your heartaches. He wants each of us to come to Him, to know Him personally.

God is so rich in mercy, and he loved us so much, that even though we were dead because of our sins, he gave us life when he raised Christ from the dead. (It is only by God's grace that you have been saved!)

—*Ephesians 2:4-5 (page 895)*

God loves you.

He created you in His image. His desire is to be in relationship with you. He wants you to belong to Him.

Sadly, our sin gets in the way. It separates us from God, and without Him we are dead in our spirits. There is nothing we can do to close that gap. There is nothing we can do to give ourselves life. No matter how well we may behave.

But God loves us so much He made a way to eliminate that gap and give us new life, His kind of life—to restore the relationship. His love for us is so great, so tremendous, that He sent Jesus Christ, His only Son, to earth to live, and then die—filling the gap and taking the punishment we deserve for refusing God's ways.

God made Christ, who never sinned,
to be the offering for our sin, so that we could
be made right with God through Christ.

—2 Corinthians 5:21 (page 884)

Jesus Christ, God's Son, not only died to pay the penalty for your sin, but He conquered death when He rose from the grave. He is ready to share His life with you.

**Christ reconciles us to God. Jesus is alive today.
He will give you a new beginning and a newly created life
when you surrender control of your life to Him.**

Anyone who belongs to Christ has become a new
person. The old life is gone; a new life has begun!

—2 Corinthians 5:17 (page 884)

How do you begin this new life? You need to realize

…the necessity of repenting from sin and turning
to God, and of having faith in our Lord Jesus.

—Acts 20:21 (page 849)

Agree with God about your sins and believe that Jesus came to save you, that He is your Savior and Lord. Ask Him to lead your life.

God loved the world so much that he gave his
one and only Son, so that everyone who believes in him
will not perish but have eternal life.
God sent his Son into the world not to judge the
world, but to save the world through him.

—*John 3:16-17 (page 811)*

Pray something like this:

Jesus, I do believe you are the Son of God and that you died on the cross to pay the penalty for my sin. I agree with you about my sin and I want to live a life that pleases you. Enter my life as my Savior and Lord.

I want to follow you and make you the leader of my life.

Thank you for your gift of eternal life and for the Holy Spirit, who has now come to live in me. I ask this in your name. Amen.

God puts His Spirit inside you, who enables you to live a life pleasing to Him. He gives you new life that will never die, that will last forever—eternally.

When you surrender your life to Jesus Christ, you are making the most important decision of your life. Stonecroft would like to offer you a free download of *A New Beginning*, a short Bible study that will help you as you begin your new life in Christ. Go to **stonecroft.org/newbeginning**.

If you'd like to talk with someone right now about this prayer, call **1.888.NEED.HIM**.

Who Is Stonecroft?
Connecting women with God, each other,
and their communities

Every day Stonecroft communicates the Gospel in meaningful ways. Whether through a speaker sharing her transformational story, or side by side in a ministry service project, the Gospel of Jesus Christ goes forward. In one-on-one conversations with a long-term friend, and through well-developed online and print resources, the Gospel of Jesus Christ goes forward.

For nearly 75 years, we've been introducing women to Jesus Christ and training them to share His Good News with others.

Stonecroft understands and appreciates the influence of one woman's life. When you reach her, you touch everyone she knows—her family, friends, neighbors, and co-workers. The real Truth of the Gospel brings real redemption into real lives.

Our life-changing, faith-building community resources include:

- *Stonecroft Bible and Book Studies*—both topical and traditional chapter-by-chapter studies. Stonecroft studies are designed for those in small groups—those who know Christ and those who do not yet know Him—to simply yet profoundly discover God's Word together.

- *Outreach Events and Service Activities*—set the stage for women to be encouraged and equipped to hear and share the Gospel with their communities. Whether in a large venue, workshop, or small-group setting, women are prepared to serve their communities with the love of Christ.

- ***Small-Group Studies for Christians***—these studies engage believers in God's heart for those who do not know Him. Our most recent, the Aware series, includes *Aware, Belong*, and *Call*.

- ***Stonecroft Life Publications***—clearly explain the Gospel through stories of people whose lives have been transformed by Jesus Christ.

- ***Stonecroft Prayer***—foundational for everything we do, prayer groups, materials, and training set the focus on our reliance on God for all ministry and to share the Gospel.

- ***Stonecroft's Website***—stonecroft.org—offering fresh content daily to equip and encourage you.

Dedicated and enthusiastic Stonecroft staff serve you via Divisional Field Directors stationed across the United States, and a Home Office team overseeing the leadership of tens of thousands of dedicated volunteers worldwide.

Visit **stonecroft.org** to learn more about these and other outstanding Stonecroft resources, groups, and events.

Contact us via **connections@stonecroft.org** or **800.525.8627**.

STONECROFT
stonecroft.org

Books for Further Study

Baxter, J. Sidlow. *Explore the Book*. Grand Rapids, MI: Zondervan, 1987.

Chafer, Lewis Sperry. *Major Bible Themes*. Grand Rapids, MI: Zondervan, 1974.

Eims, Leroy. *The Basic Ingredients for Spiritual Growth*. Wheaton, IL: Victor Books, 1992.

Enns, Paul. *The Moody Handbook of Theology: Revised and Expanded*. Chicago, IL: Moody Publishers, 2008.

The Expositor's Bible Commentary. Grand Rapids, MI: Zondervan, 1976.

George, Elizabeth. *A Woman's Walk with God*. Eugene, OR: Harvest House Publishers, 2000.

Graham, Billy. *The Holy Spirit*. Nashville, TN: Thomas Nelson, 2000.

Lloyd-Jones, D. Martyn. *Life in the Spirit: In Marriage, Home, and Work—An Exposition of Ephesians 5:18–6:9*. Grand Rapids, MI: Baker Book House, 1973.

MacArthur, John. *The Keys to Spiritual Growth*. Wheaton, IL: Crossway, 2001.

———. *The Silent Shepherd*. Colorado Springs, CO: David C. Cook, 2012.

Martin, Glen, and Dian Ginter. *Drawing Closer*. Nashville, TN: Broadman and Holman, 1995.

Ryrie, Charles C. *Basic Theology*. Chicago, IL: Moody, 1999.

———. *The Holy Spirit*. Chicago: Moody, 1997.

Strauss, Lehman. *Galatians and Ephesians*. New York: Loizeaux Brothers, 1957.

Swindoll, Charles R. *Flying Closer to the Flame: A Passion for the Holy Spirit*. Charles R. Swindoll, Inc., 1993.

———. *He Gave Gifts*. Plano, TX: Insight for Living, 1998.

Stonecroft Resources

||||||||||||||||||||||||

Stonecroft Bible Studies make the Word of God accessible to everyone. These studies allow small groups to discover the adventure of a personal relationship with God and introduce others to God's unlimited love, grace, forgiveness, and power. To learn more, visit **stonecroft.org/biblestudies.**

Who Is Jesus? (6 chapters)

He was a rebel against the status quo. The religious community viewed Him as a threat. The helpless and outcast considered Him a friend. Explore the life and teachings of Jesus—this rebel with a cause who challenges us today to a life of radical faith.

What Is God Like? (6 chapters)

What is God like? Is He just a higher power? Has He created us and left us on our own? Where is He when things don't make sense? Discover what the Bible tells us about God and how we can know Him in a life-transforming way.

Who Is the Holy Spirit? (6 chapters)

Are you living up to the full life that God wants for you? Learn about the Holy Spirit, our Helper and power source for everyday living, who works in perfect harmony with God the Father and Jesus the Son.

Connecting with God (8 chapters)

Prayer is our heart-to-heart communication with our heavenly Father. This study examines the purpose, power, and elements of prayer, sharing biblical principles for effective prayer.

Prayer Worth Repeating (15 devotions)

There is no place where your prayers to the one and only God cannot penetrate, no circumstance prayers cannot impact. As the mother of adult children, your greatest influence into their lives is through prayer. *Prayer Worth Repeating* is a devotional prayer guide designed to focus your prayers and encourage you to trust God more deeply as He works in the lives of your adult children.

Pray & Play Devotional (12 devotions)

It's playgroup with a purpose! Plus Mom tips. For details on starting a Pray & Play group, visit **stonecroft.org/prayandplay** or call **800.525.8627.**

Aware (5 lessons)

Making Jesus known every day starts when we are *Aware* of those around us. This dynamic Stonecroft Small Group Bible Study about "Always Watching and Responding with Encouragement" equips and engages people in the initial steps to the joys of evangelism.

Belong (6 lessons)

For many in today's culture, the desire to belong is often part of their journey to believe. *Belong* explores how we can follow in Jesus' footsteps—and walk with others on their journey to belong.

Call

Every day we meet people without Christ. That is God's intention.

He wants His people to initiate and build friendships. He wants us together. *Call* helps us take a closer look at how God makes Himself known through our relationships with those around us.

Discover together God's clear calling for you and those near to you.

Order these and other Stonecroft Resources at our online store at **stonecroft.org/store.**

If you have been encouraged and brought closer to God by this study, please consider giving a gift to Stonecroft so that others can experience life change as well. You can find information about giving online at **stonecroft.org.** (Click on the "Donate" tab.)

If you'd like to give via telephone, please contact us at **800.525.8627.** Or you can mail your gift to

Stonecroft
PO Box 9609
Kansas City, MO 64134-0609

STONECROFT

PO Box 9609, Kansas City, MO 64134-0609
Telephone: 816.763.7800 | 800.525.8627 | Fax: 816.765.2522
E-mail: connections@stonecroft.org | stonecroft.org

Notes

1. J. Sidlow Baxter, *Explore the Book* (Grand Rapids, MI: Zondervan, 1987), pages 154-155.

2. Elizabeth George, *A Woman's Walk with God* (Eugene, OR: Harvest House Publishers, 2000), page 8.

3. Adapted from Charles C. Ryrie, *The Holy Spirit* (Chicago: Moody Publishers, 1997), page 125.

4. Charles Swindoll, *Insight for Living* radio program, broadcast of June 22, 1999.

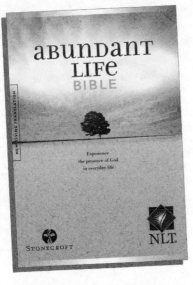

Abundant Life Bible
New Living Translation
Holy Bible

*Experience the presence of God
in everyday life*

Stonecroft is pleased to partner with
Tyndale to offer the New Living
Translation Holy Bible as the
companion for our newly released
Stonecroft Bible Studies.

The New Living Translation translators set out to render the message of the original
Scripture language texts into clear, contemporary English. In this *translation*, scholars kept
the concerns of both formal-equivalence and dynamic-equivalence in mind. Their
goal was a Bible that is faithful to the ancient texts and eminently readable.
The result is a translation that is both accurate and powerful.

TRUTH MADE CLEAR

Features of the Abundant Life Bible

- Features are easy-to-use and written
  for people who don't yet know Jesus
  Christ personally.

- Unequaled clarity and accuracy

- Dictionary included

- Concordance included

- Old Testament included

- Introductory notes on important abundant life
  topics such as:

Gospel presentation	Practical guidance
Joy	Life's tough issues
Peace	Prayer

- Insights from a relationship with Jesus Christ.

- Ideal Scripture text for those not familiar with
  the Bible!

 Tyndale House Publishers

To order: stonecroft.org/store
800.525.8627

 STONECROFT
stonecroft.org/SBS